Your DESTINY is in your HANDS

CHIZOBA IHEZUKWU a.k.a Chizzy

 A catalogue record for this book is available from the National Library of Australia

Copyright © 2019 Chizoba Ihezukwu

All rights reserved. No part of this publication may be reproduced, stored in a retrieval system, or transmitted in any form or by any means, electronic, mechanical, photocopying, recording or otherwise without prior permission of the author.

Publisher:
ASPG (Australian Self Publishing Group)
P.O. Box 159, Calwell, ACT Australia 2905
Email: publishaspg@gmail.com
http://www.inspiringpublishers.com

National Library of Australia Cataloguing-in-Publication entry

Author: Ihezukwu, Chizoba

Title: **Your Destiny is in Your Hands**/*Chizoba Ihezukwu*

ISBN: 978-1-922327-19-2 (print)

ISBN: 978-1-922327-20-8 (eBook)

TABLE OF CONTENTS

Dedication 5

Acknowledgement 6

Introduction 7

Chapter 1: **WHAT IS LIFE** 9

Chapter 2: **DESTINY** 13
    Anger 19
    Fear 20
    Guilt 24

Chapter 3: **MAINTAINING A GOOD LIFE** 27
    Happiness 27
    Motivation 29
    Positive Thinking 32
    Faith 33
    Prayers 37

Chapter 4: **TWO THINGS IN LIFE** 42
    Accept situations and conditions
    as they manifest themselves 42
    Take responsibility to change your situation 43

Chapter 5: **FULFILLED LIFE** 47
    Glorifying the Name of God 47
    Adding Value to People 50
    Give God Your Concerns 52
    Experience God's Wholeness in Your Life 54

DEDICATION

This book is dedicated to God almighty for His never-ending grace, infinity mercy and opportunity given to me from the start of this book to the end. Even in my lowest moment, God guides me through.

ACKNOWLEDGMENT

This project would have been impossible without the support of my lovely children, husband, Mum, brothers and sisters for their emotional and physical support.

I would like to thank Patricia Gauci, Rev. Fr. Peter for their extraordinary support during this journey. I will not forget to remember Pastor Francis, Bro. Eneh Gordian Nnamdi and Uju Ebenye for their immense support and spiritual advice.

For those who have contributed one way or the other in my life, I really appreciate all you have done, you all know yourself.

INTRODUCTION

Life can be so challenging, only people with strong will and mind can succeed in this life. You have the power to create and mould your life the way you want it to be. Stress cannot be eliminated entirely from our present-day society, but you can decrease how you allow stress to affect your day to day activities by seeing every stressful and painful situation as an opportunity to grow.

I realize through my stressful moment that so many people in this world are going through the same situation and life experience with different issues that is beyond their power to control, so many of them are not as lucky as some people to come out of it very strong. Something shifted for me, I started thinking about the leading cause of mental health in our society and only answer I can find is STRESS and PAIN. Human life is like a season, a season to cultivate and to reap what you sow. God allowed the season to come to taste your faith. To pick up your pieces, don't blame anybody for your predicament, secrete to life is to find solution to your problem and move forward from your past because it's history.

God created us in His own image and likeness, it is His intensions for us to enjoy life to the fullest but most times we are the cause of our problem, remember God does not count our past sins to bless us. When you are in pain, search yourself and listen to nature talking to you, maybe there is something God is trying to convey to you, all successful people find their purpose in an awkward position, if they can do it, I believe you can do it as well. Just believe in yourself, trust God and marry your bible because bible has all the answer to every situation.

The intension of this book is to go wide to help people going through one problem or the other to sit up and fight back at life because life is not going to be easy and smooth as you planned but if you persevere everything will work out for you.

Chapter 1
WHAT IS LIFE

Life is nothing but a misery, try very hard to unfold it; it is full of inconveniences, but it is too short to worry about irrelevant things. Sit up and take control of your life, enjoy life to the fullest no matter what you are going through, life is like an onion you have to peal one layer at a time and sometimes you cry, don't allow anybody or any situation to take your joy or happiness from you. Everybody in this world has something they are dealing with, it could be grief, having the feelings of hopelessness or worthlessness, being rejected, having an addiction or sickness. Life is everything depending on the way you are looking at it, everybody has different experience in life and that shapes our vision about life and who we are but no matter what your life experience is, remember that somebody loves you and that somebody is Jesus.

I am talking out of experience because I am a victim of circumstance; I thought my world was coming to an end, I allowed the pressure of society to get to me. However, when I realised that my happiness and destiny does not rely on any individual or even society, my perspective about life changed, I now see myself as the daughter of the Most High God, since then I occupy the driver's seat of my life. I want to use this medium to help people going through hard times especially youth and young adults to remember that all hope is not lost, hang in there, owe your life and go after what you want, all the equipment you need to achieve your dreams is inside of you, just activate it by concentrating fully on yourself and know exactly your purpose of existence, keep the right attitude and know that somebody is watching. Again, that somebody is Jesus; he knows about you and loves you. Keep going he will wipe away your tears one day. There is nothing difficult for God to do, whatever happens in your life God knows about it, He will not allow any difficulty to befall you if he doesn't want to use it for your own good. In the book of *Jeremiah chapter 1 vs 5, God said," before you were born, I already know you by your name"*, meaning that whatever that is going on in your life is part of the process for God to use it to glorify His Name. Keep thanking God and glorifying his name even when you are having difficulties. Most times God is using your present condition to get you closer to your destiny. Remember Zacchaeus the taxi collector in the bible Lk 19: 1-9, he was a notorious sinner, and everybody hated him, but God chose to eat in his house that is to tell you that God's way is not our way. Zacchaeus life changed from that moment, he tried to refund those he took their things and became a new creature. People can choose to criticize or condemn you; criticism is not always a bad thing, depends on the way you take it. In life, you cannot control what people say or do because everybody is entitled to their own opinion, but you can control how you respond. Nobody is above criticism, avoid it if it is irrelevant, or you learn from it, if it is constructive. Joseph in the book of Genesis 37, his brothers hated him, they called him a dreamer and sold him off to the Egyptians, they thought they had eliminated him for good but indirectly it was the beginning of his journey to his destiny. Joseph story shows that God is ordering his steps for his dream to come to reality because his brothers wanted to kill him when they saw him coming but Reuben intervened and told them to put him in the dry well so he will rescue him later but as they were eating Judah suggested, they should sell Joseph to Ishmaelite and they all agreed, he was sold for twenty pieces of silver to the Ishmaelites who took him to Egypt even though Joseph suffered in the hands of his master's wife and was sent to prison but at last God used him to glorify His name, our life is strategically planned by God, nothing happened by chance, if God have not finish with you, nothing is going to harm you no matter the gravity of the obstacle on your way, it is just your own route to your destiny. My point is that you are God's favourites, your present condition is not your conclusion, when you are down with something, God is up to something. God chooses who to bless even when you are in a critical situation and feel like there is no hope of coming out of it. Remember miracles happen to those who persist, if you don't stretch yourself, you will not receive so quit sitting around blaming yourself or people around you. Don't give too much attention to what you cannot change, release the toxins of life.

Your Destiny is in your Hands

If you give space to guilt, you will not have the confidence you need to move forward, out of your pain can come your purpose. You are in charge of your life and your decisions determine your successes and consequences. Sometimes it looks like you are alone, but no you are not, God is with you and God wants you to concentrate on yourself and find your inner self, sometimes God will take things or people away that we think we need to succeed in life so we can depend on Him and not people. If people are not there, you don't need them to fulfil your purpose, you only need God. Having too many friends around you can be a distraction to God's plan for your life. For you to be great in life, you must limit your friends, so you will have quiet time to think and communicate with nature, reflect with your life and connect with your future purpose of existence and try to follow those you learn something from. You are not defined by your past, you are defined by your present so set goals and go after them with all determination because success is connected with action. Successful people never stop moving forward, they make mistakes, but they never quit, don't be afraid of making mistakes because through mistakes you learn, take correction and grow from it. The choice is yours, you can be a host to God or a hostage to your ego.

Chapter 2
DESTINY

Destiny is simply your purpose of existence because nobody is born into this world by mistake, you were created to achieve your full potential. *In the book of Ecclesiastes chapter 6 verse 10 says, whatever exist has already been named, and what humanity is has been known, no one can contend with someone who is strong.* Human beings have whatever they need for their existence inside of them, it is our responsibility to connect with our inner beings to become what we are created to be. Nobody is greater or better than anybody, your gift is special and that makes you who you are, don't try to be like another person because everybody have unique destiny for human consumption, no human being are the same in this world but were created in God's image and so no destiny is the same because people have their unique way of manifesting their destiny in a way that is best known to them and that makes them who they are. To achieve your destiny, you will have so many obstacles in your way. The purpose of these obstacles is to build and modify you for the next level. Sometimes people will attempt to talk you out of your destiny but remember you are the only one feeling what you are feeling from the inside so keep calm, concentrate on yourself, listen to your spirit, walk by faith and not by sight to attain your full potential, *for the revelation awaits an appointed time, it speaks of the end and not prove false. Though it lingers, wait for it; it will certainly come and will not delay (Habakkuk 2:3).* Don't wait to have it all before you start doing something because it will never happen, while waiting for God's favour, keep working on yourself for improvement, no matter how small, God cannot do it all for you because he entrusted everything you needed inside of you before your creation to achieve your full potential. In the book of Jeremiah, God calls you what you were before you were born, and no human being can take that away from you, sometimes what people want to use to bring you down is what God uses to lift you up, no obstacle can change God's plan for your life but you must work for it, nothing in this world comes easy. All of our destinies are different, some people will know and understand their purpose on earth from when they are children. Some people will learn their destiny along the way, while some will like to shy away from their destiny because they are not comfortable with it. If you find your purpose later in life, never mind, it is never late to start pursuing your dreams, don't say you are too young or too old to achieve your dream, life destiny is different in every individual. Don't limit yourself to your environment because so many people in that environment have started living their dream life with what they have. Don't think about quitting because you are uncomfortable, as this is part of the process to get you to your destiny. God uses the preparation process to put us where he wants us to be. Remember Jonah in the bible, God wants him to go to Nineveh but instead he decided to go in another direction because he was not comfortable with the assignment. However, God used that situation to glorify His name by putting him inside the fish mouth for three days and on the third day God made the fish to drop him on the country he was originally meant to go to and so Jonah finished the assignment. God can put many obstacles in your way to push you where He wants you to be or give you set back to get you prepared. God does this, not to destroy you but actually for your own good. Sometimes it doesn't make sense to us but at last we will understand why it happened,

> *the book of proverb 20:24 says a person's steps are directed by the Lord. How can anyone understand their own way? Your script of life has been written by God who directs your steps so don't feel bad when something happens in your life.*

Because it is the creator's way of getting you closer to your destiny, remember your life history have already written by God from the day you were born to the day you will go back from earth, it will not be easy but keep your trust in God and keep working towards your dream because you have something special in you that needed to be developed or bring to reality. Remember your destiny is in your hands, don't settle for less, you own your life so drive yourself around the way you want. Our future can be nurtured, taken care of and bring to reality by ourselves, it is you that can guide and shape the route your journey takes. Don't fall to enemy's threat, telling you, you will never move beyond your limit, enemy uses those lies to strike fear and anxiety in our hearts, don't let fear to overtake you but instead listen to that tiny voice telling you, you can do it. Push yourself to destiny through God's word, His promises and power of the holy spirit to channel your vision the direction you need to move in your life. God never forget His promises, keep reminding Him of his promises. Take kids for example, when you promise something to them, you will try to fulfil your promise because for kids, promises are an unbreakable law. A man promised to buy a pair of shoe to his child, though he doesn't have the money at the moment but each day that passes by the child kept reminding his father about the pair of shoes, telling him but "you said" you will buy me a pair of shoe, holding his father by his word, he bought the shoe for the child. His father bought the shoe so that the child will leave him alone and to fulfil his promise. This is exactly how our father in heaven operates, it is not that God is forgetful or wants us to keep reminding Him, but it is to strengthen our faith in God. Bible tells us to have faith like a child, the child never have a doubting mind that his father will not buy his pair of show, he believe his father must fulfil his promise, he kept his faith in his father knowing that his dad must fulfil his promise to him. Keep reminding God with quotation from the bible relating to your problem, God must surely answer you to fulfil His promises. Again, in the book of Mark 6: 23-29, Where the daughter of Herodise danced for Herod and he asked her to request for anything she wants and he will do it for her, she requested for John the Baptist head in regards of her mother's choice. Herod granted her request even though it was against his wish and very difficult for him to fulfil the promise, but he has made the promise in front of everybody. If herod can go as far as offering John's head to keep his promise, how much more our father in heaven. God will never abandon or forsake us in our time of need. Keep praying and reminding God of His promises. Reminding God of His promises will make us to remain faithful and trusting God in all we do and also reassures us of God's endless mercy. God wants us to live our dream life, never give up when things are not working in your direction, it is just a test of faith. Don't be overwhelm with your present circumstance, present your case with prayer to God, He will surely answer you to fulfil His promise in your life, remember what God told us in the book of Isaiah 43:28, "present your case to prove you are in the right". Eg of how to present your case to God, There is this couple that married for 18 years without any issue to show for the marriage, they kept their faith and believe that one day God will bless them with fruit of the womb, the man is a prayer warrior, he prays and help people around him to find favour in the hands of God but he couldn't pray his way out, they have prayed, went to chapel, nothing changed for them. One day they decided to change their prayer pattern by holding God by His word. They wrote a note with different bible quotations reminding God where he said that there will be no barren among your children, they both signed it and present it to God in prayer. (According to them, they told God, we are presenting our case to you, you told us in the book of Deutronomy 7:14 and Exodus 23:26, no woman in your land will be miscarry or be barren. God we are your children, we have tried everything to have baby, but we don't have baby). They kept remind God of His promises till after 18 years of marriage, God fulfilled His promises in their life, and they had triplets, two boys and a girl. Who will believe that after 18 years of marriage that this couple will still have kids but God kept His promises in their life. God has a purpose for your life so don't go to God on the basis of your need instead go before God based on His purpose for you. When you pray, remind God of His promises, hold Him by His words, that burning destiny in your heart is not for your happiness but to glorify the name of God. Pray and have faith that it will come to pass.

> *In Philippians 4:6-7, Do not be anxious about anything but in every situation by prayer and petition with thanksgiving present your request to God. And the peace of God which transcends all understanding will guard your heart and your mind in Christ Jesus.*

It is very essential to avoid anger, fear, and guilt to reach your destiny because they will deprive you of happiness and isolate you from the social world. If care is not taken, you may end up with depression or even mental illness. Remember life is too precious to waste so guard your own very carefully. Let's have a quick look on how Anger, Fear and Guilt will affect your destiny,

Anger

Living in anger will deprive you of joy. Anger is a natural feeling of pain due to bad circumstances and it is manifested in the heart. Anger is not necessary a bad thing but when it is too long, it can cause damage to our well-being so anything you don't have control over, forget about it and move on because it did not happen by mistake and is not worth your stress. It is your destiny to be like that, most times it helps us to find our innermost self, out of your pain can come your purpose so don't allow your pain to deprive God's blessings in your life because God has his unique way of getting us to our dream life, don't be carried away with pain because your pain produce your purpose.

> Psalm 37: 8-9 says don't give in to worry or anger; it only leads to trouble. Those who trust in the Lord will possess the land, but the wicked will be driven out.

By letting go of anger, you will begin to take control of your life, be at peace with yourself and live a normal life like every other person in spite of your circumstances. Nothing in this world is perfect, everybody has their own baggage so don't blame yourself. You can't do anything about the past, but you can do something now and your future. Anger can lead to so many physical illnesses, like insomnia, causing you not to sleep while others are sleeping at night, remember the shorter your sleep, the shorter your life. It increases the risk of having a heart attack, high blood pressure and stroke.

I am pointing this out because it is better to start practising a healthy lifestyle than to dwell in self sorrow and anger, looking for someone to blame. Remember your happiness is in your hands, you can choose to be happy or angry. Though sometimes we can't avoid anger or stress, it is ok to be angry for a short while but if it gets too long, it can cause damage to our health so practice exercise, relaxation technique and counselling anytime you are angry, it will help you to be calm and re position yourself. Again, it will be better to voice your anger to the person and let them know how you are feeling, sometimes it helps to calm the nerves and you find out the reason behind the action;

> *if you stay calm, you are wise, but if you have hot temper, you only show how stupid you are. Peace of mind makes the body healthy, but jealousy or anger is like a cancer (Proverb 14: 29-30).*

control your emotions and do away with anything that can compromise your joy and live you to anger. Define yourself the way you know best, being angry is a choice, it depends on what you want in life. Living in anger can make you to find fault in everybody around you, just to make yourself feel better.

Fear

> *Joshua 1:9 says, "Remember that I have commanded you to be determined and confident. Don't be afraid or discouraged, for I, the Lord your God, am with you wherever you go".*

When you believe in your ability to do something, remove all the side attraction, work towards achieving your goal, it determines your success but as human beings, we don't normally see our potentials rather we concentrate on people's opinion about us and see ourselves as people see us but it doesn't have to be like that, God knows what we have in us and told us to be determined and confident, remember He is always with you and know exactly what you are doing at a particular time so don't allow anybody to tell you what you can or can't do because you destiny is in God's hand and no human being can stop God's plan for your life except you. Sometimes our greatest obstacle to reaching our destinies is fear. Fear can make you hide behind excuses. For instances, fear of social gatherings can make one to give excuses only to avoid the function, but the issue is after hiding behind excuses, the problem is still there. So instead it affects your happiness and ultimately increases the fear. Often the fear will increase, which can lead to isolation and depression. At times we give up on what we want to do in life because of what will happen on the way, fear of what people will say or fear of the past. It is important to forget the past and focus on the future; you cannot live with past regrets and strive towards future happiness. Fear we created in our mind. Most times fear does not exist, it could be our imagination or how we feel, don't allow fear in our mind to push us around otherwise we will not achieve our goals or reach our full potential. Fear is one of the devil's most popular weapon to attack us which will put us into perpetual agony, most often fear subject people into depression and anxiety. I was a prisoner of my life for so long, I don't always feel excited going out, I always wants to stay indoors even though I was not originally a going out person but I reduced going out from the things I normally like to do, waiting for things to change but it never did till I change my thinking and re mould myself and start seeing what life has to offer, whatever you are going through in this world, never give up in life and never stop enjoying your normal routine as usual. Before you succeed in life, you will fall before you rise, listen to the story of all successful people, they all fall and some of them fall many times before they become who they are, don't stay where you fall instead keep pushing yourself till you get to where you want to be because success is hidden inside hard work and discipline. Nature has its way of communicating with us, underneath your fear listens to nature talking to you. Those people that overcome their fear are able to reach their full potential. To overcome fear, know that you are unique and special, there is no other you. Put your shoulders back, start carrying yourself with confidence because you are fearfully and wonderfully made. Don't allow fear to kill your sense of reasoning by making you to be stuck in life. So many people died without reaching their potential due to fear, that is why the greatest or the richest place on earth is a grave yard so fight back and make a difference, listen to nature and start developing your dreams because you are not a biological mistake, you are here on earth on purpose, there is something needed on earth that God hide inside you. God trusts and depends on you to carry out the assignment he entrusted in your care. Don't give excuses or try to blame somebody for your predicament but try to be focused and work on yourself, you can never learn a gift rather you refine your gift because your gift is the source of your value. Your wealth, education, all your achievements are just material things acquired to make your life easy, but they will never add value to your life, your value comes from your gift. For example, a boy of 24 years old committed suicide and reason was unknown to people but the most interesting part is that the boy has everything at his disposal, when people look at him, they thought he is very lucky because of acquired wealth but there is something lacking inside this boy that make him to take his life, material things will not do what the sense of value will do for him and this situation is rampant in our society today where the rich people always end their life and reason unknown, even youth and young adults, most times people around us are going through difficulty and in most cases, some of them are good in hiding their feelings to their friends and even their parents till they finally succeeded in killing themselves. Have you ever asked yourself, why those educated, rich people commit suicide and die? Because of fear of the unknown, they feel dissatisfied with the position they find themselves, they feel they are not valued, hopeless, useless and depressed, they feel they are lost in life, in most cases they will want to end it and leave this wicked world, so many teenagers and young adults commit suicide in this present time due to fear of cyber bullying or one problem or the other and they lose interest to continue with life because nothing in this world moves or gives them joy again. Regardless of what you are going through in life, don't blame anybody for making you feel the way you are feeling, because nobody can hurt your feelings without your permission, your feeling comes from your thoughts so take full responsibility and change what you don't like around you because you can do it. Learn how to develop personal relationship with God to overcome any obstacle in your way because you will begin to see things through His eyes, and one with God is a majority. *"Acts 17:27 says God is at work in everyone's life"*. If God is still at work in our life. Don't you think you have all the ability to transform your life the way you want it to be? Each day is a brand-new day and something new is happening in our life. If we know the power and ability that are under our control, we will shape the world, but fear is stealing those power away from us. Fear limits vision and lack of self-esteem, it will make you to stop believing in your abilities, your talents and your self-worth by preventing you from pursuing your goals and expanding your life, fear can prevent you from taking risk. Fear only addresses our emotional thinking but not our rational thinking, to live a healthy and successful life, we must learn to control our emotions so we can push past our fear to accomplish more in life.

Guilt

Feeling guilty can affect our self-esteem and stop us from progressing in our emotional and physical life. Feeling guilty is a natural part of the healing process but becomes unhealthy when it goes on for too long. Guilt will deprive you of the confidence to move forward and steals your joy, you will start seeing yourself as others sees you but instead see it as an avenue to re-examine yourself and correct your mistakes. Remember your opinion about yourself matters, not what people thinks about you and feeling guilty will keep you from improving yourself.

> 2 Corinthians 5: 17-18, Anyone who is joined with Christ is a new being; the old things have gone, the new has come. All this is done by God, who through Christ changed us from enemies into his friends and gave us the task of making others his friends also.

God does not keep record of our sins, he understands that we are mere mortal, whatever you are feeling guilty about, bring it to God and he will forgive you all your sins so stop worrying yourself about things you don't have control over, learn from your mistakes and move on with your life. Moving on does not mean pushing aside your feelings but rather accepting your flaws and works towards changing it to something positive. Your value is based on the fact that you are a child of God. God created you in His own image and likeness so rise and take the pressure off your shoulders, start seeing the good things life can offer. Life is not about owing explanation to people or impressing people for you to be happy. You and only you hold the key to your happiness, only you can unlock your happiness. Feeling guilty can confuse or paralyse your emotions by causing you to be ashamed and regretful throughout your life, stop from feeling guilty by accepting it's in the past now, you can't change the past and ask yourself what is the way forward because you have the power to do something from now moving forward, look for new possibilities and explore yourself to make things better in future. God does not look at our past mistakes to bless us, but He looks on what we are doing now. He is very much aware of your present condition, He allows it because He knows you can handle it. Trust God to take you through this journey called life by making peace with Him and allowing Him to come into your life and take control of everything concerning your life. When I was in that position, I was consumed with myself, I have so many things going on inside of me, I kept telling myself, "where did I go wrong", so this is how my life is going to end, who did I wrong; I am a failure because I have failed my family and my parents, but little did I know that it is a way of God calling me to use myself to tell others to wake up from their slumbers, when life is happening to you, it will not make sense initially but as time goes on, you begin to understand why it happened. Thank God every time in your life where you are and where He is taking you to.

Chapter 3
MAINTAINING A GOOD LIFE

Maintaining a good life is very essential in everything we are doing in this life because if you are healthy, you will be able to concentrate in achieving your dream and to do that, eat healthy, do physical exercise, above all; below are things that can help you go miles and live your dream life.

   a. Happiness
   b. Motivation
   c. Positive thinking and
   d. Faith and
   e. Prayer. PUSH

Happiness

It is our duty to fill our life with happiness which is the essence of life. Life is full of ups and downs, everybody has one or two things they are dealing with, nobody is free from the complications of life except the little children that enjoy their life anywhere they find themselves. As we grow older, we start looking for what to accomplish or start comparing our lives with others. Whatever that is going on in your life, make happiness your priority because happiness is a choice, associate yourself with what you enjoy, give yourself a treat and make friends with those that make you laugh. Happiness reduces stress and pain, helps us to live longer, to be more productive and increases our creativity and they are always in their right sense when making judgement, they are optimistic and have confident in themselves and always full of energy to identify their strength and also make a commitment to achieve it. Being happy will attract people or friends around you because happy people have the power to motivate, encourage and put smile on the faces of people around them, they tend to live a healthy and successful life because they live in the moment and are grateful. Happy people also go through life challenges, but they chose not to dwell on it or put enough energy on their problem. As human beings, we all want to be happy but most times it is a struggle to find happiness because we are looking at the wrong places for happiness. The only person that can give us inner happiness is God. *Psalm 144:15, happy are the people whose God is the Lord, and also in Psalm 146:5, happy are those who have the God of Jacob to help them and who depend on the Lord thy God.* If you want to succeed in life, embrace God and trust him to ride you in this wonderful journey called life because he will never make mistake in directing your steps. If we commit ourselves to God fully, He will take full responsibility and complete care of our life in every angle even when we are the reason for our problem.

Motivation

Motivation simply means how excited we are in pursuing our happiness and it is the reason for our action. Sometimes, due to circumstances or tragedies of life (unpredicted life event), it kills our motivating spirit, we withdraw from our drives and become stagnant. Everybody's reason for existence is different, that is the reason we have different drives to our happiness. Some people are motivated by going to space, some inspiring the world, some are creative. All these shows that we have different purpose in this world, so search your inner self and find who you really are (Self). Unpredicted life events happen but don't dwell on them, see it as a reason to move forward, sometimes what we are passing through in this world is a way of God directing us on our purpose of existence. If we are not motivated or being depressed about something, we will not have the energy to move forward or pursue our dreams. Motivate yourself, no matter what the obstacle is, be resilient because if you don't push yourself in this life, you will be stuck and keep dwelling on your past or blaming people for your failure. Failure happens and people with strong mind and persistent scales through, life will not give you everything you need on a platter of gold, you must dig deep and fight your way through before you achieve your purpose. Look at the great people you are seeing today, they experienced difficulties, but they kept pushing, that is why you are hearing about them today. Never give up the dream you want to develop, because it is your purpose of existence, nobody can do it better than you so keep motivating yourself and one day you will be in a position you want to be. To be successful in life, you need a skilful mind and ability to perform. Some people lack this quality in their life, they thought life is about competing with people , trying to get people listen to their own side of story, you don't need anybody's approval for you to be successful, all you need is trust and believe in yourself, if others can do it, why can't you? This life is just a mindset, how you view it and what you want it to be for you. Keep a positive mindset, trust and embrace God to see you through.

When I was growing up, a friend of mine, from a wealthy family, all her siblings studied to the level they wanted to, most of them travelled abroad to finish their education but this my friend managed to finish secondary school and her parents wanted her to continue but she refused, saying she wants to pursue her dream and her parents asked "what do you want to do", and she told them she wanted to be a tailor but they refused, calling her all sorts of name, that she wants to bring disgrace to the family. Uncles and aunties were involved in talking some sense into her, but she refused. They reluctantly allowed her to do what she wants. Today this lady is doing marvellously well; she has a very big boutique with workers she pays a salary. Who knows what would have happened if she had listened to her family and went for study, maybe by now she will be struggling in life, finding her place in this world, but instead she is a well-respected proud business owner.

She has a very strong motivation with strong will which helps her to know exactly what she wants and follow her heart's desire, because it is what drives her and gives her inner satisfaction. Sometimes, we feel trapped and don't want to go with our motivation because of what people will say, to please our parents or scared within ourselves. Those things are not accountable, forget any side attraction and continue pursuing your dream, it is the reason for your existence, but it will never be easy unless you persevere and be resilient to push yourself through. Motivation is like somebody that wants to lose weight, keep postponing the action to lose weight like exercise, eating healthy, the person will not lose weight but when the person practices exercise and start seeing results, the person will have the motivation to keep doing what he was doing for better result; that is exactly what happens in our everyday life, if you don't motivate yourself, believe you can do it, dedicate, put your time, persevere and push yourself to the next level, you will be stagnant and be resentful of everything around you but when you try and push yourself, you will start seeing good results and that will motivate you, give you more energy and strength to keep pursuing your purpose of existence; don't wait for things to get better before you start doing something because it will never get better unless you start changing the things around you, remember a journey of a thousand miles begins with one step, start gradually and all other things will come into place.

Again, let someone you trust know about your motivation, by so doing you are obligated to fulfil your promise because somebody is looking up to you to deliver.

Positive Thinking

Positive thinking will help you to create thought and bring it into reality. It come with energy and enthusiasm that drives your mindset towards achieving the inevitable. Why is it that some people will set their mind to achieve a goal but couldn't and other people will have a difficult task to accomplish, at the end they will come out with positive result. Difference between positive minded people and negative minded people is that, positive thinking people always have the ambition that they will change their situation no matter the circumstances and even change the world at large. They will put their time, their energy and everything within their limit to make sure that they bring their dream to life and they will never sleep unless they achieve their purpose, but the negative minded people always succumb when they fail and never want to try again. Look at the people that make it in life today, it's because they persist and never stop on the way, for instance the computer we are using today, somebody produced it, television, phone, air plane is people's creativity because they have positive mindset. My dear, God created you in his own image and likeness and He put you in this world for a purpose, you are not in the world by mistake, God has a purpose for you and wants you to fulfil your destiny. Those people that produce computers and so on are human beings like you, they don't have two heads, but they found their purpose on earth and use their positive attitude to fulfil their destiny. What are you waiting for? You have all it takes to push yourself, wake up from your slumber, quit putting accusing finger on people about your predicament, you have the power to change what you don't like around you, just apply the law of nature and put on positive thinking, you will see yourself thriving. By law of nature, I mean listening to the purpose of God for your life, sometimes nature speaks to us by pushing words into our ears but in most cases, we ignore it because we belittle ourselves thinking that the task is so much, we will not be able to accomplish it. Everybody is unique in his or her own way and our gifts are different, don't put down your purpose of existence and keep wallowing in pain, if you don't abide by the law of nature, you will be lost and life will be meaningless, whatever you are going through could be a way of God to channel you to your purpose of existence. Don't ignore, embrace it and have a positive mind towards it and you will see what God will use you to do.

Faith

With faith we can do the unthinkable. *In Hebrew 11:1 faith is the assurance of things hoped for, the conviction of things not seen.* We believe things through faith, we believe that Jesus Christ came to the world and suffered for our sins, even though we have not seen Him, but we believe. Verse 29, we believe through faith that the Israelites crossed the red sea as if on the dry land and when the Egyptians try to cross the red sea, water swallowed them up. We believe all the miracles in the bible through faith and believe it could happen in our own time, that is why we pray to God for our needs and believe he will answer our prayers because of faith, but sometimes as human beings, we have doubt and that is where our problems start. Peter in the book of Matthew, walked in the water through faith when Jesus appeared to them, but became distracted and started sinking, Jesus rescued him and asked him why did you have doubt?, when God is with you, you don't need to be afraid because faith and fear don't go together, sometimes, our circumstances can be so drowning but never mind, God controls all the storms in our life, just trust in God's timing, in the presence of your storm, keep looking unto Jesus, never be distracted because God is the author and finisher of our faith. God has mapped out your root, path it will follow and way of escape if you are stuck, just trust and obey His commands, maintain your faith in Him and God will take you to next level in your life because faith unleashes the supernatural. A little faith in God can change your life permanently,

> Matthew 17:20 I assure you that if you have faith as big as mustard seed, you can say to this hill, go from here to there and it will go. You could do anything.

Faith is the only weapon in life that put you in any position you want to be in life, faith and fear don't get along, where there is fear, faith will disappear and you will start doubting yourself and stop believing because of fear and it will hold you back from seizing any opportunities that comes your way, don't doubt your ability in trying new things, step out and try to take risk, life is all about risk and at some point in life people have self-doubt but for successful people, they don't let the feeling of doubt stop them from moving forward. Always be yourself, have faith in yourself, among all keep trusting God if you want to attain the highest level in your life, keep God first in everything you are doing, allow God to take control of your life, direct your path and put you in the position you want to be in life and when God finishes his work in you, you will always have an endless happiness that comes from the inside. It is only God that can give you eternal happiness, then why are we doubting God? Don't you think that if God can make Peter to walk on the sea as if it is dry land, He is in control of all our circumstances? We get stuck in fulfilling our dreams because we doubt or question our ability. Let me tell you, you can do whatever you set your mind to do in this life, if you decide you are going to be a prime minister (President of a country) and you believe in yourself fully without doubt and work towards it, then follow the law of nature, the sky is your limit. Determination is the key to life. Have you asked yourself why some people make it in life and others don't? The answer is because the winners believes in themselves and pursue their dreams even with the obstacles on their way, they overcome them and bring their dream to reality while the losers hide in their shell when they have obstacles and live their life exactly where they are stuck. Next thing you will hear from them "is how God wants it". This is not true, God wants you to live your dream life. He created you with a vision of what He wants you to accomplish, that is why everybody you see is different and unique in their own way. If you believe it is how God wants it in your life, how did other people succeed in life and your own case is different? Because those people that succeeded persevere and keep pushing themselves through life and have faith that one day, they will come out with something tangible as proof of it. Look around you, everything you see that helps in human existence is somebody's dream, the toys, the chairs, television, bed, park, fan, air plane and so on, if those people hide in their shadows, we wouldn't be where we are today. For example, I know I want to touch lives and help people to live their fulfilling life, and be the voice to the voiceless and less privileged but I don't know where to start, initially I told myself, who are you? Why do you think you can do it? How do you think you can do better than those people that are doing it already? In the middle of my confusion, I told somebody about my dream and how I want it to come to reality but the answer I got was, "so many people are doing that already", do you think your own will be different from what others are doing? And for me to succeed, I must do extraordinary things from what others are doing. The answers I got put me on the edge to pursue my dream for a very long time, but one thing I vividly know is that I am not happy with my current position in life. I decided to do something about my life, within me I know I am not on the right spot for my life and I decided to start with this straight away because I believe it will help most people around the world to wake up and start pursuing their dreams. You never know what your body can do until you try yourself. Believe in yourself, trust that your dream will make a difference when it comes to reality. Have faith in God who put those dreams in you to see you through to the end. If you have faith and believe in yourself, you will never fail even in difficulty or even when people are trying to look down on you. To make a change, challenge yourself and push yourself to the extreme to make things happen then you will experience the fulfilling happiness in you. God can use you to do wonders if you are determined, persevere with faith and push yourself through life, and remain convinced in your heart that God will keep his promises because He created us to bring Him glory and to do that is by being the person, He created us to be.

Prayers

Prayers and faith work hand in hand because prayer deepens your faith and helps you to understand very well God's purpose for your life. If Jesus Christ can start with prayer and end with prayer to fulfil His purpose on earth, who are we not to follow His footstep. Prayer is the key to successful life, for you to reach your full potential, you need to have an intimate relationship with God and to do that, pray in season and out of season, trust in God's timing and His plan, He will use you to change the world. Prayer builds rapport between you and God and pushes the heaven's gate to open for you if you abide with God. Look at Hannah in the book of 1 Samuel 1 and 2, she and her co wife Peninnah married to

Elkanah, Peninnah had children while Hannah was childless, she prayed with her heart and God answered her prayer and bless her with a child, again Jabez prayed for God to bless him and enlarge his territory, God answered him and made him king if God can answer him and change his situations, Jabez which simply means pain because his mother gave birth to him in pain, apparently, the pain is still following him and he prayed to God to change the situation, God will change your situation if you trust in him.

> *John 16:24, You have not asked for anything in my name until now; ask and you will receive, so that your happiness may be complete.*

Jabez asked and he received, likewise so many people in the bible. Remember that God created us in His own image and likeness, if He can answer and do miracles in the olden days, what do you think have changed, that make him not to answer our prayers and use us to do miracles as He did in the time of Abraham? The answer is simple, sin and again we don't have enough faith to trust God in our difficulties. For instance, our father on earth hears and attend to our needs accordingly, he doesn't want anything to happen to us, always pray for us to be better than them. Imagine what will happen to us if we embrace and trust God as our personal lord and saviour, He will open the door of favour on us and use us to do miracle as He did in the time of Abraham. Our God is a merciful and compassionate God. He knows you have those gifts and talents in you, but He wants you to do the right and necessary things for you to activate your potential, prayer and hard work are the highest force to unlock your potentials. God gave us everything at our disposal, but you must work for it before it becomes reality. With prayers, you will have the spirit and mind to bear whatever life throws at you. It will help you to be closer to God and have the right as the son or daughter of the Most High God to shake heaven, because you and your father are friends, and one with God is majority. Jesus prayed relentlessly when He was in the world because He knew the key to life and use it to defeat all the temptations that came his way. People are suffering in the world today because they don't know who their father in heaven is, that is why people are committing suicide, doing all sorts of atrocities because they don't want to be in this life again. Nothing you see in this world is greater than what Jesus passed through when he was on earth, 2000 years ago when Jesus Christ was in the world, he was betrayed by his friend Judas Iscariot for 30 pieces of silver, nobody believed him, they all wanted to crucify him and release the prisoner, even Peter denied him three times before the cock crow, Jesus Christ was in pain to the extent he prayed to God to take the burden out from him, but he persevered, take all the punishment for our sin, he used his weapon (Prayer) to overcome them all. If Jesus Christ the Son of God can go through scare for our sake, nothing we are going through will compare what Jesus went through in his own time so don't allow your scare to disqualify you from fulfilling your purpose. God can use you to do the same work as Jesus; if you can trust Him, believe in Him and know that he put you in this world for a purpose, however you came in this world does not matter, the only thing that matters is that God wants you in this world to do the assignment He gave you to do, so that the world will be a better place, don't look at the circumstances around you, He who put that dream in you, knows how to make it come to reality, just believe and do your path by working in yourself and see God doing wonders in your life.

In the book of Psalm 30 verse 5 "Tears may flow in the night but joy comes in the morning", this moment of difficulty could be your night when everything you are doing is going wrong, it is not your fault but it is called life because it has its ups and downs, remember your morning is coming very soon, don't sit and wait for things to turn around, you must put effort to change your situation if you are not comfortable with it. Despite all the challenges of life, it has its unique way of bringing out the potential in us. Don't let people hold you back with your past to keep you from moving forward because you were who you were and now you are who you are and you suppose to be cool with both of them, don't regret any of them because God is aware of your situation and knows that those things will happen before they happen, He is very much aware that we are human beings, the only thing he wants from us is to recognise our sins and beg for forgiveness, remember the woman caught in adultery in the book of John 8:1-11, people wanted to stoned her to death because she committed adultery but Jesus Christ bent over and wrote on the ground with his finger and said, if you have not sinned, cast a stone at her, but before he raised his head, the whole people had gone and he said to the woman go,

I have forgiven you but don't sin again. God does not look at your past sins to bless you, the Mary Magdalene who was healed from evil spirits and infirmities by Jesus was the first to see Jesus when he rose from death, that is to show you that our God is a merciful God, you must not be a saint for him to accept and bless you. The scripture says, "do not be afraid of those who will kill only the body but always be afraid of those who will kill the body and soul. The secret of life is perseverance, take Jesus as an example, He passed through tribulations but because He knew where he was going, he endured it and persevered to the end. It doesn't matter what happened to you, what matters is what you are doing about it, don't allow your emotions to control you. Take for instance, in this present time, people are committing suicide, some result in mental illness, while some have one health issue or the other due to one problem or the other, let go, you cannot change anything by thinking but you will be accumulating your problem, you have only one life so guard your own. I am talking out of experience because I allowed myself to be drowned in pain but inside my pain I can feel nature talking to me on how to use my situation to help others wallowing in pain, I was denying it, but it kept coming. Take full responsibility of your life, accept where you are and take yourself where you want to be, nobody will do it for you except you.

Chapter 4
TWO THINGS IN LIFE

There are two things in life that can make us to become who we are created to be or losing out from our purpose of existence. When we become who we are created to be, we are advocate of Christ because we are not accepting our present predicament rather, we channel our energy to our value, and when we fall and remain stagnant, we are losing out from the purpose of existence. They are:

 a. Accepting situations and conditions as they manifest themselves or
 b. Take responsibility to change your situation

Accept situations and conditions as they manifest themselves

When you accept situation as they are, you will never progress, rather get stuck in life, always complaining to people to feel sorry for them. If you cannot change your present predicament, forget about it and move on, don't live in the past but live in the present, people treat you the way you treat yourself, if you add value to your life, people will start treating you with value. For instance, when people dress like mad people, they will be seen in the same category as a mad person. You are not the only person life adversely affected, those people you are complaining to, have their own story also to tell, stop playing a victim. One thing about life is that it has its ups and downs, you could be happy today and tomorrow sad, it is up to you to decide the position you want to be in, enjoy your life now and make your blue print known to the world because you are in this world for a purpose, you have talents and goals, so pursue them and make a difference, for if you don't, you will remain angry and suffer because of the decisions you make and when you are gone from this planet the world will suffer it. You have the power to recreate yourself, decide to live each day as it is the last day, invest in yourself. Your life and happiness are the most important thing so stop wasting time in changing your situation to suit the way you want it to be.

Take responsibility to change your situation

Taking responsibility of your life helps you to know how to respond to challenges of life and moves you from becoming a victim to a victor. To do that, accept responsibility for your actions and failures which will help you to develop in life, make peace with God and also accept criticism in a positive way, don't take it personal, correct your weak points, concentrate on the present and forget about the past because past is history. Most times, people dwell in their past and holding themselves hostage, forgetting that people also make mistakes in life both young and old, accept where you are and be happy where you are going. You owe yourself, your thoughts, thinking, actions, feelings and words and when you realize this, you will never hand the driver sit of your life's journey to anybody, you will be able to know that your life and happiness is in your hands, in every moment of your life, the choice is yours. When you take responsibility to change your situation, you will start to have inner confidence, believing in yourself, have the abilities to do something or fulfilling a task and have a positive mindset that things will work out.

Your life, your story, there is nothing you are going through now that supersedes what Job went through in the bible, he lost everything he had, his wife and his friends rejected him but at last he regains everything because he trusts and believe in God. Why we are having problem is because most times we try to solve our problems ourselves. Even though Job's life had been turned upside down, He lost everything he had, his loved ones, his friends, all his wealth and his health, Job was frustrated but he kept his faith and keep trusting God in the most critical time of his life. How do we take challenges of life today? Nobody wants to have patience and trust God to do His work in our life. Most times we start asking God questions, "why did you allow this to happen to me? "and keep reminding Him all the good work we have done and how we help the less privileged". God knows all those things even before you open your mouth to remind Him. It is very easy to trust and believe God when things are moving well with us, but when things go wrong in our life, we get frustrated, start accusing God, some will go and find solace in the hands of a doctor (native doctor) thereby compounding their problem. God wants us to trust and believe in Him in the most critical stage of our life.

> *In the book of James 1:5 he encourages us to ask God for wisdom in our trials and tests because through the process of trials and test our true faith is strengthened and the quality of our character is developed.*

God wants us to grow, so "He allows us to undergo through trials and tests to stimulate our growth (John 15: 2)". Sometimes, it doesn't make sense to us why we are in difficult situations and it makes it very difficult for us to accept the suffering. In other for God to bless us, we must endure hardship with patience to prove our faith in God because trials in our life do not necessarily mean punishment for our sins, but it is the devil's way of manipulating us to think God does not care about us. When you are in the night days of your life, embrace God and trust Him to hold your hand through the pain and make a way for you where there is no way to overcome the pain. In other words, we must help ourselves because God will not single-handedly lift you from your struggle, you must contribute to overcome your obstacles and by doing so, see yourself beyond the circumstances, keep putting effort and continue telling yourself;

"I am blessed and highly favoured and I can do this". Take risk to change your situation, because if you don't, you will not grow and become your best which will affect your happiness and when you are not happy, you are ruined for the rest of your life. Which means there is a tendency of jeopardizing your physical and emotional health, thereby causing havoc to your existence.

Chapter 5
FULFILLED LIFE

In Philippians 4, He tells us how to live a fulfilled life, in his book, He has four stages to live a fulfilled life which are,

   a. Giving God the glory.
   b. Add value to people.
   c. Bring your concerns to God and
   d. Experience God's wholeness in your life.

Glorifying the Name of God

Philippians 4:4 says may you always be joyful in your union with the Lord. Always glorify God in every condition you find yourself. When you are going through difficulty in life, remember that creator of heaven and earth are very mush aware of your predicament, don't get frustrated, anxious, or insulting the name of the Lord but put all your petition in prayers with thanksgiving present your request to God. When you celebrate God, He will manifest himself with full force in your life to rise above the obstacles.

> *Be joyful always, pray at all times, be thankful in all circumstances. This is what God wants from you in your life in union with Christ Jesus. Do not restrain the holy spirit or despise inspired messages. 1 Thessalonians 5:16-20.*

To glorify God, always honour Him in your thoughts and actions, learn to love one another without hypocrisy, keep God's commandments, serve others as Jesus did when He was in the world, spread the gospel of the Lord. David in the bible constantly praising the name of God even when he falls short of glory of God. To give God all the glory, repent and confess all your sin to him, God does not need your money or food, He only need a pure and contrite heart, take for instance, Cain and Abel in Genesis 37 when they offer their thanksgiving to God, Cain was a farmer and Abel was a shepherd. Abel killed and gave the best part of the first lamb born of one of his sheep as a sacrifice to God while Cain's sacrifice was rejected, and God was pleased with Abel's offering. Cain was very angry about that and one day, Cain told Abel lets go for walk, Cain killed his brother at the countryside. Abel used his heart to appreciate God by giving Him the best of what he had. He understands that all he got came from God. Given God gift or offering at the church is always Good but God is not interested in them rather He is interested in our soul, all God wants is our pure heart, be at peace with one another, never look down on your fellow human being because everybody is equal in the sight of God. Remember to look after the less privilege, have faith in God, worship God in truth and spirit, acknowledge God in all you do. All the glory goes to God and not human being. God will manifest his power in your life if you give him all the glory no matter where you find yourself, even in your trial keep glorifying God because He must surely show His power over your life. Sometimes, miracle will not happen immediately but if you keep your faith and look unto Jesus, things will turn around for you. For instance, There is this business man, he was selling electrical parts, each time people come to buy parts in his shop, they will tell this man to increase the amount in the receipt so that their master will not know how much they bought it but this man kept refusing and told them it is against his faith, they stopped going to his shop to buy goods , this man was suffering because he cannot sell his goods, all because he kept his faith in God and vow never to put his hand in such business, at a point, he find it difficult to feed his family, he couldn't pay his children's school fees but kept managing till when God turned his position around. Those people that wanted this man to falsify his receipt finished serving their master and got settled to start on their own. As time goes on, they employed their own servant, so what they do now is when they send them to buy electrical parts, they direct their servant to this particular man that refused to falsify his receipt because they know that if they buy it from the man, they will not steal because the man will put them exactly the price he sold the goods on the receipt. But because this man kept his faith in God, even though it was not easy for him and his family, but they believed that God will never forsake them. His prayer was answered, and all those waisted years were recovered. Now this man and his family are living like a king.

Adding Value to People

A life worth living is worth living good (for others). For you to live a fulfil life is to live for others. There is joy and fulfillment in adding value to people's life. You can add value in people's life through words of encouragement, helping the needy, giving people listening ear without looking down on people, promote people's dream and give them hope, accept people you meet in your life for who they are and don't be judgemental because nobody is perfect, compliment people in your life, you never know who you are inspiring, people are good at smiling outside but inside they are weary. Weariness can cause people to be discouraged from living their dream life. If you find yourself in a privileged position, thank your stars but remember that wealth is not for your own consumption only, God gave them to you for a purpose. The reason why God put you in a privileged position is to look after those that are under you. Today what do we use our wealth to do? Do we use it to glorify God by looking after the less privilege people around us or do we use it to crucify the less privilege and subdued them to worship you? Matthew 25: 35-40 when you feed the poor, look after a stranger, sick people or visit the prisoner, you did it for me, if you see yourself among the privileged, God put you in that position to glorify His name by looking after those that don't have any clothe to put on, food to eat, people that are going through one thing or the other, use your privileged position to worship God. There is post I got on my phone where a young man was helping a man with his six children, none of them in school and his wife was dead for two years back and no money to bury her, they barely eat and live in an uncompleted building, according to the young man, a friend of him sent the video of this man and his kids to him, he was touched so decided to help the man and his children, he rented a good appointment for them furnished it, make sure the children start school, gave them money to bury their mother, also told the man to look for business he will like to do, so he will give him money to start the business. This is adding value to people's life in authentic way, without any ulterior motive. There are so many ways of adding value to people's life, it is not only by monetary terms but by making people feel happier, by making them feel important, unique and special, by helping them in such a way that their problems will appear smaller or help to enhance their dream and give them hope. Paul says in the book of Acts of the apostle, 20: 35,

> *'I have shown you in all things that by working hard in this way we must help the weak, remembering the words that the Lord Jesus himself said, there is more happiness in giving*

Again, Jesus Christ added value to people's life by watching the feet of his disciples intentionally to show us what humility is all about. God added value to human kind by breathing life into him and provide everything needed for human being to succeed, without him, we are nothing and to crown it all Jesus Christ died for our sin so that we may have life in abundant. Add value to people in your life, it attracts all sorts of fulfilment that can never be bought we money.

Give God Your Concerns

The problem we are having in this present time is carrying our problem on our shoulder without consulting the creator of the world. *Proverb 3:5-6, trust in the lord with all your heart, and do not lean on your own understanding.* In all your ways acknowledge him, and he will make your path straight. The same God yesterday, today and tomorrow, God never changes, He uses people to do miracle in the bible to glorify his name. He will still do it again if we call on Him, trust and believe he will do it, he will do wonders but some people don't recognise God in everything they do and they are finding it difficult to overcome challenges of life because at some point in life, we all go through struggle so keeping God first at everything you do, will enable God to direct your path even when your situation is so critical. Most times, people will try to think of ways to maneuver their way around obstacles with their own strength, they forget about their father in heaven, who created everything with his own mouth, try always to consult God in your difficulties and trust him for strength and wisdom to overcome them all. In the book of John 14 from 13,

> *And I will do whatever you ask for in my name, so that the father's glory will be shown through the son. If you ask me for anything in my name, I will do it.*

Through prayer we obtain favour from God but it doesn't mean that everything we ask from God must be granted because God knows exactly what we need at a particular time, He answers our prayers but sometimes it is not what we expected, we see what is happening now but God sees beyond the physical and answer us accordingly. When I was in critical moment of my life, I was very confused and don't know what to do because things are not moving in my life as they should, I tried all my best to change the situation but it kept getting worse by the day, at a point, my mind was very blank thinking forward how to come back to life again, I was in the middle of nowhere when my friend called me, she noticed from my voice that I was not happy, after several questions, she told me there is nothing God cannot do, I told her yes I believe that God can do all things but to me I don't see my current situation necessary to start putting it in prayers because I do pray every day. After that conversation, I changed my pattern of prayer and took charge of my life, I put everything in prayer and specifically bring my present concern to God, everything about me changed, I started seeing life as it should be, I don't keep everything to heart anymore, I concentrated more on myself, live at the moment, I started seeing people's behaviour as their problem not mine, my life changed automatically and started enjoying inner peace. God is the only one that can give you inner peace, trust and believe in Him, you will experience His power in your life.

God can change your life if you bring all your concerns to him, but each time we want to do it by ourselves, he will step back and wash you, always remember that God is greater than every situation you are passing through, consult him and he will lead the way. *In the 1 Cor. 10:13, "every test that you have experienced is the kind that normally comes to people. But God keeps his promise, and he will not allow you to be tested beyond your power to remain firm, at the time you are put to test, he will give you the strength to endure it, and so provide you with a way out".* When God allows life to visit you, he knows very well, you are capable to endure it and to remind us that our home is not in the world, that real life begins in the after life which is heaven. Appreciate God in your pain and know that you are highly favoured to be chosen, pain has a way of bringing us close to God. Pain always has a purpose, and, in every pain, there is always an opportunity. It also helps those that have passed through pain to give hope to the hopeless through their own situation. One problem with human beings is that everybody wants to give testimony, but nobody wants to go through tribulation before having anything to testify.

Experience God's Wholeness in Your Life

We cannot achieve a very good amount of change or wholeness in our life with our strength and abilities when we keep God on the sideline. It is only God that can transform us to achieve wholeness in our life, put God first in your life and allow him to take his position in your life to transform you.

Proverb 16:3 says Ask God to bless your plans, and you will be successful in carrying them out.

Never give up in life whenever you fail, keep pushing and trust in God, always remember that everything in this world are systematically planned accordingly by the creator, so does the condition you are in today, nothing in this world happened by mistake, God knows about it and most times those difficulties are happening to open door to our destiny. When you are in pain, it is your choice to be a victor through your pain or a victim, the choice you make when you are in pain determines the quality of life you will have, either you shape your destiny by yourself or you let fate shape it for you, every choice we make reflects our past, determines the outcome of our future and destiny. I was a prisoner of my own life for more than six years, without knowing the answer or how I will set myself free from the bondage, I was not happy, I kept blaming everybody around me. I kept finding fault in everybody, little did I know that I am doing those things to make myself feel better, I was waiting for things to come back to normal without contributing anything to make it happen, during the period of waiting I realize that the hardest test in life is the patience to wait for the right moment. In life, if you want to have a good life, you must work very hard to achieve your goal.

inside my pain, I can feel nature talking to me, but I don't want to listen to nature because it very stressful for me, the day I accepted to do something in my life, was the day my life changed automatically, I started seeing life with a whole new dimension, I started seeing people as they really are, without judgement or criticism. Pain can complicate your life, change your body system and even your sleeping pattern, pain comes with headache, fatigue, muscle pain and lack of concentration to push yourself forward. I was at the edge of loosing my life to physical condition before I entrust my problem to God. Stress can drain us physically and mentally, stress is inevitable, we cannot run away from it because life happens and the way we handle stress differs from one individual to another. Pain/stress can make you to reach your full potential or it destroys you, but the decision is yours. If other people can find their purpose out of their pain, why can't you? Why are you trying to take short cut? In life, there is no short cut. Most people today have cut their life short because of pain and they think is too much for them to handle. The most common cause of suicide among our young adult in our society today is because of stress/pain. Committing suicide is not an ideal way to respond to our difficulties but to be resilient, keep pushing forward and never give up in life, among all remember that God is the author and finisher of our faith (Hebrew 12:2), put all your trust in him because nothing in this world is difficult for God to handle. God only wants to test our faith in him for the favour He is about to release in our life. If the hair of our head is numbered by God (Matthew 10: 29). How do you think that God will forsake you, He knows everything concerning your life so bring all your problem to God and watch God's miracle manifesting in your life. Suicide is not an option because it will never solve your problem rather it brings perpetual agony to the people you left behind and you are not sure where your soul will be after committing suicide so be careful, open up your problem to people to find help. A young boy in his teen committed suicide, still in secondary school, his parents and friends did not noticed any changes in his attitude, he normally go to school and come back like every other kids, each time they finish there evening routines in the house, the boy will go to his room, that fateful night, after having dinner with the family, they all said good night, the young boy went to his room and kill himself with chemical substance, his parent was surprised because they did not see it coming, be vigilant with people around you and assist help when needed. Life has so many good things to offer and you have a very big future ahead of you, you never know if you will become prime minister, governor or a very prominent person in the society. You can transform your life and become whatever you want to become, just concentrate in developing yourself and stop worrying about life experience, remember everything you need to become whatever you want in this world is inside of you though it is not going to be easy but as a human being, we have unlimited potentials, other people did it in the past and thrive to their full potential, so why can't you channel your energy in developing you instead of dwelling in self sorrow and wanting to take a short cut by contemplating suicidal thought. Sometimes, if we start feeding our emotions with negative thoughts, it results in most developing mental illness. Take very good care of your mental statues and stop feeding the negative thoughts in your brain.

This wonderful world called life can be amazing and bitter, things happens for a reason, accept the fact that it happened to teach us a lesson and to encourage us to grow to next level in our life. Inspire and motivate yourself through this journey of life, take control and be the driver seat of your life, through your story, you can inspire and motivate people because everybody has a story to tell and nobody will tell your story more than you. All of us are potential human beings with hidden treasures and endless possibilities. Trust, believe and never relent and you will see yourself transform to another level in life. Don't wait for ideal time because it will never be ideal, life waits for no one, time waisted is long gone, get up and pursue your dream and stop blaming people for your predicament. One thing is for sure, you don't have to get it all to get started, start wherever you are, don't wait for big stage before you start doing something, start with your pen and paper, use your phone depending on what your dreams are, put at least 30 minutes of your time every day to fulfil your dream life, remember you don't have to be great to get started but you have to get started to be great. If I can do it, I believe you can do it as well. Sit up, challenge yourself and pursue your dream, you will see tremendous change in your life. God have not finish with you and His plan in your life is irrevocable.

www.ingramcontent.com/pod-product-compliance
Lightning Source LLC
Chambersburg PA
CBHW071545080526
44588CB00011B/1798